I0759476

POCKETBOOKS

by BroadStreet

100 Bible Promises for Boys

BroadStreet KIDS

BroadStreet Kids
Savage, Minnesota, USA
BroadStreet Kids is an imprint of BroadStreet Publishing Group, LLC.
Broadstreetpublishing.com

100 Bible Promises for Boys

9781424571604
9781424571611 eBook

Entries composed by Cayla Roy.

Typesetting and design by Garborg Design Works | garborgdesign.com
Editorial services by Michelle Winger | literallyprecise.com

Printed in China.

26 27 28 29 30 31 32 7 6 5 4 3 2 1

God says...

Introduction

This book is filled with God's words for you. Short, powerful verses from the Bible will remind you how much God loves you and is always with you—no matter what.

Perfect for bedtime, quiet time, or anytime you need to feel God's love, this small book is great to keep close wherever you go.

You are strong, you are brave, and you are loved by God. His promises are forever!

1

God Is Your Strong Tower

The Lord is like a strong tower.
Those who do what is right
can run to him for safety.

PROVERBS 18:10 ICB

When you feel afraid, you can pray to God and ask him to protect you. He is like a big, strong tower. He will keep you safe.

Thank you, God, for being a strong tower that keeps me safe!

2

God Gives You Peace

"I leave my peace with you.
I give my peace to you."

JOHN 14:27 NIRV

When you have big feelings that you don't understand how to control, pray for peace. Tell God what is on your heart today. He loves you and gives you his peace!

God, thank you for the peace you give me.

3

God Has Good Plans for You

"When I plan something, it happens. I do the things I want to do."

ISAIAH 46:10 ICB

God has plans just for you, and they are good. When God plans something, you can be sure that it will happen. He planned for you to have life, and now you do! Ask God what else he has planned for you.

I thank you, God, for all you have planned for me.

4

God Teaches You

God, you have taught me
since I was young.
Even until today I tell about
the miracles you do.

PSALM 71:17 ICB

Ask God when you don't understand something. He will teach you. He wants to tell you about the wonderful things he does. Ask him, and he will help you learn.

God, please teach me every day of my life.

God is with you.

5

God Blesses You

Give praise to the God and Father of our Lord Jesus Christ. He has blessed us with every spiritual blessing.

EPHESIANS 1:3 NIRV

God promises to bless you with all that you need. He will take care of you. How great is that? Praise him for all he has blessed you with.

God, thank you for all the blessings you have given me.

6

God Gives You Rest

"Come to me, all you who are tired and are carrying heavy loads. I will give you rest."

MATTHEW 11:28 NIRV

When you are tired or worried, God will take care of you. Run to him. He will comfort you and give you rest.

Thank you, God, for the rest you give me.

7

God Gives You Eternal Life

"God so loved the world that he gave his one and only Son. Anyone who believes in him will not die but will have eternal life."

JOHN 3:16 NIRV

God loves you so much that he wants to be with you forever. If you believe in Jesus, you will live forever in God's kingdom.

Thank you, God, for sending your Son and for giving me eternal life!

8

God Will Give You Life

"Honor your father and mother. Then you will live a long time in the land."

EXODUS 20:12 ICB

When you choose to do what your parents tell you to do, you are honoring them. When you say good things about them instead of bad things, that is also honoring them. God wants you to honor your parents. And when you do, he will give you life!

God, please help me to honor my mom and dad.

God listens
to you.

9

God Cares for You

Give all your worries to him,
because he cares for you.

1 PETER 5:7 ICB

God cares for you so much. He wants to hear about all of your worries because he loves you. Spend extra time with God today and tell him what is on your mind. He cares about whatever it may be!

I am so glad you care for me, God.
I care about you too!

10

God Gives You What You Need

My God will meet all your needs.

PHILIPPIANS 4:19 NIRV

If you ever worry about what will happen tomorrow or the day after that, pray. Ask God for what you need. He may answer in different ways than you think, but he knows what is best for you. He will give you what you need.

I am grateful, God, that you give me what I need.

11

God Gives You Grace

God is full of grace. From him we have all received grace in place of the grace already given.

JOHN 1:16 NIRV

God will be patient with you. He is always waiting for you to come to him. He loves you so much that his arms are open wide for you to run into. He will comfort you with his grace.

Thank you, God, for the grace you have given and will keep giving me.

12

God Loves You

We love because God first loved us.

1 JOHN 4:19 ICB

God loves you so much! He loves everything about you. He made you to love others. Show some of God's love to people today by doing something nice or saying something kind.

I thank you, God, for loving me so
I can love others.

God gives
you peace.

13

God Makes You Strong

Those who trust in the LORD will receive new strength.

ISAIAH 40:31 NIRV

No matter what happens, you can depend on God. When you fall, he will pick you up. When you cry, he will comfort you. When you feel sick, he will heal you. When you are afraid, he will bring you peace. He makes you strong!

I thank you for the strength you have given me, God.

14

God Is Fair

Many people want to be heard by a ruler.
But fairness comes from the Lord.

PROVERBS 29:26 ICB

Sometimes you might beg your parents or your teacher to listen to your side of the story. You think they will make things fair. Did you know that fairness comes from God? He will listen, and he will always be fair.

God, help me to give my worries to you. Thank you that you are always fair.

15

God Is Your Safe Place

The LORD will watch over your life
no matter where you go,
both now and forever.

PSALM 121:8 NIRV

Have you ever been afraid? Do you know that God can keep you safe? He will watch over you and protect you. The next time you are afraid, pray to Jesus! He will keep you safe.

Thank you, God, for always protecting me and for keeping me safe.

16

God Heals You

Lord, my God, I prayed to you.
And you healed me.

PSALM 30:2 ICB

God made your body so well, it can heal itself when you are sick. If you are sick right now, pray and ask God for healing. He will take care of you.

God, thank you for healing me when I am sick.

God wants you
to be with him.

17

God Understands You

The LORD gives wisdom.
Knowledge and understanding
come from his mouth.

PROVERBS 2:6 NIRV

When you are having a bad day and it feels like no one understands you, you can trust that God does. He will give you wisdom and show you what to do. Ask him what lesson he wants you to learn when you are having a hard day.

God, thank you that I can always count on you.

18

God Will Guard Your Heart

Don't worry about anything. No matter what happens, tell God about everything.

PHILIPPIANS 4:6 NIRV

You are a child of God. He loves and protects your heart. He will make sure to guard it and keep it safe. Put your faith in him and trust that he will keep you from all evil.

God, I trust you. Thank you for guarding my heart.

19

God Loves You Very Much

The Lord loves us very much.
His truth is everlasting.

PSALM 117:2 ICB

God smiles when he sees you. He loves you so much. You are a treasure to him. He wants to play with you and share the world with you. He is kind and loving.

God, I am thankful for your love. You are so kind to me!

20

God Is Your Friend

"I call you friends because I have made known to you everything I heard from my Father."

JOHN 15:15 ICB

God is your friend! He loves spending time with you. He is with you all the time, even while you play, eat, and sleep. He loves every minute he gets with you. In good or bad times, you can trust that God is your friend!

I am so grateful to have a friend like you, God!

God has a place
for you.

21

God Gives You Mercy

God shows mercy where he wants to show mercy.

ROMANS 9:18

God forgives you. This is how much he loves you. Even when you have done something wrong, you can ask God to forgive you, and he will show you mercy. He loves you so much more than you can understand.

Thank you, God, for how much you love me.

22

God Is Your Hero

The Lord protects my life.
So why should I be afraid?

PSALM 27:1 ICB

Do you know Spiderman, Superman, Batman, or another superhero? God is more powerful than all of them! He has saved you from the biggest enemy in the universe, and he loves you very much. You know a superhero. How cool is that?

I am so grateful I have you as my hero. I love you, God!

23

God Hears You

If we ask anything in keeping with what he wants, he hears us.

1 JOHN 5:14 NIRV

God knows all your wants and needs because he hears you. No matter what, he listens to you. He wants to hear you call out to him. Talk to God today. You can trust that he is listening.

God, thank you for hearing me and for giving me what I need.

24

God Guides You

*"I will always guide you.
I will satisfy your needs in a land
baked by the sun."*

ISAIAH 58:11 NIRV

When you are not sure what path to take, God will guide you. He will show you what is right and what is wrong. All you have to do is trust in him and follow him wherever he goes.

I am so grateful that you guide me, God.

God makes you strong.

25

God Comforts You

"I comfort you because of who I am."

ISAIAH 51:12 NIRV

Whether you are sad, afraid, or something bad has happened, you can trust that God will comfort you. He loves you so much and wants you to feel safe. If you feel bad today, ask God to comfort you and believe that he will.

Thank you for the comfort and peace you give me, God.

26

God Is Your Strength

The Lord is my strength and shield.
I trust him, and he helps me.

PSALM 28:7 ICB

God is so strong and powerful. When you feel weak or tired, you can depend on his strength to help you. God also gives you power over your mind. If you feel stuck in anger or sadness, you can ask God to give you self-control.

God, thank you for the strength you give me every day.

27

God Watches Over You

The Lord will keep you from
every kind of harm.
He will watch over your life.

Psalm 121:7 NIrV

God knows how you feel. If you have a bad dream or see something that scares you, you can ask God to keep you safe. He will! Call out the name of Jesus, and he will protect you.

Thank you, God, for always keeping me safe.

28

God Makes You Clean

If we confess our sins, he will forgive our sins. He will make us clean from all the wrongs we have done.

1 JOHN 1:9 ICB

God sent his Son, Jesus, to die on the cross for your sin. Whenever you lie, don't listen, or do something bad, you can ask God to forgive you, and he will make you clean.

Thank you, God, for making me clean from sin.

God keeps you safe.

29

God Helps You Win

He protects me like a strong, walled city.
I will not be defeated.

Psalm 62:6 ICB

God is so strong! You can always rely on him to help you win. He protects you and keeps you safe. With him on your side, you will always win!

God, thank you for helping me win my battles.

30

God Is Close

The Lord is close to everyone
who prays to him,
to all who truly pray to him.

Psalm 145:18 ICB

Wherever you are, God is close. He wants you to be close to him. Talk to him. He is with you all the time, and he loves that!

Dear God, thank you for always being with me.

31

God Will Make You New

Our bodies are becoming weaker and weaker. But our spirits are being renewed day by day.

2 CORINTHIANS 4:16 NIRV

Every day God is making your spirit stronger. He has given you new life. Even as you get older and weaker, you can trust him to make you new.

God, thank you for making my spirit new.

32

God Will Keep You Going

Turn your worries over to the LORD.
He will keep you going.

PSALM 55:22 NIRV

Sometimes you have strong emotions of anger, sadness, or worry. God will be there for you in those times. He will always hold you up. You can depend on him to keep you going.

God, thank you for keeping me going.

God is your helper.

33

God Knows You

You created the deepest parts of my being.
You put me together inside my
mother's body.

PSALM 139:13 NIRV

God created you, so he knows you the best. Sometimes you might feel alone or like no one understands you. But you can trust that the Creator of the world knows you inside and out!

I am grateful that you know me so well, God.

34

God Will Answer Your Prayers

If we know that God hears
what we ask for,
we know that we have it.

1 JOHN 5:15 NIRV

God hears you. If there is anything you feel like you really need, and it is something you think God wants for you, ask him for it. Trust that he will give it to you if it's right for you. He is always listening to your prayers.

God, I am grateful you answer my prayers in the best way.

35

God Fights for You

*"You will only need to remain calm.
The Lord will fight for you."*

Exodus 14:14 ICB

God is your warrior. He will fight all your battles if you let him. You do not need to be afraid. If you are feeling sad, angry, tired, or just having a bad day, try staying calm and asking God for help. He will be there for you!

God, I am so thankful that you fight for me.

36

God Will Be With You

"The Lord your God will go with you. He will not leave you or forget you."

DEUTERONOMY 31:6 ICB

God will never leave you or forget you, he will always be with you. You never have to feel alone. God is right next to you.

I love spending time with you, God. Thank you for always being with me.

God will never reject you.

37

God Will Not Let You Fall

He won't let your foot slip.
He who watches over you won't get tired.

PSALM 121:3 NIRV

If you put your trust in God, he won't let you fall. He wants to protect you. God is always ready to catch you before you fall.

God, I trust in you. I believe that you will not let me fall.

38

God Is Your Light

"I will be your light forever.
My glory will shine on you."

ISAIAH 60:19 NIRV

You never have to be afraid of the dark because God is your light. He is always with you. You can count on him to shine his light on you and show you where to go.

God, thank you for being my light.

39

God Will Lead You in Truth

"When the Spirit of truth comes he will lead you into all truth."

JOHN 16:13 ICB

If you are having a hard time knowing what to do or knowing right from wrong, God can lead you the right way. He always knows the answer. Just ask him!

God, I am grateful that you lead me into what is right.

40

God Will Guard Your Life

The Lord will guard you from all dangers.
He will guard your life.

PSALM 121:7 ICB

No matter what, God will protect you. He is your strong tower, your light, and your peace. When you are afraid or worried, go to God and he will help you.

God, I am grateful that you always guard me.

God teaches you.

41

God Is Your Rock

*"The LORD himself is the Rock.
The LORD will keep us safe forever."*

ISAIAH 26:4 NIRV

God is your rock. That means he is your solid foundation. You can trust him because he does not change. He will be your cover during a storm and a sturdy foundation when everything around you is changing.

God, thank you for being my steady rock!

42

God Is Eternal

*The Lord is the God who lives forever.
He created all the world.*

Isaiah 40:28 ICB

God is eternal. That means he will live forever. He created you so he could be with you forever too! He loves you that much. You can be excited about your future because you get to spend it with God.

God, thank you for creating me so I can be with you forever.

43

God Can Be Trusted

"The person who trusts in the Lord
will be blessed.
The Lord will show him that
he can be trusted."

JEREMIAH 17:7 ICB

No one is perfect except God. You will make mistakes sometimes, and that is ok. God still loves you, and he will still keep all his promises. You can trust him to do everything he says he will do.

Thank you, God, for being someone I can trust.

44

God Rewards Hard Work

Work as serving the Lord and not as serving people. You know that the Lord will give each person a reward.

EPHESIANS 6:7-8 NIRV

It is good to know that God will give you a reward for your hard work. Serve God and serve the people around you. Your reward is coming.

Thank you, God, for giving me a reward for my hard work.

God is patient
with you.

45

God Is Your Refuge

"God lives forever!
You can run to him for safety.
His powerful arms are always there
to carry you."

DEUTERONOMY 33:27 NIRV

You never have to be afraid with God on your side. He wins every battle. He stands in front of you and next to you. He promises to keep you safe. Be grateful that he is your refuge. He is the strongest warrior ever!

Thank you, God, for being my refuge.

46

God Gives You Freedom

You were chosen to be free. But don't use your freedom as an excuse to live under the power of sin. Instead, serve one another in love.

GALATIANS 5:13 NIRV

God is so kind. He gives you the freedom to choose whether to do good or to sin. You can choose to love God and serve others or to be selfish and only serve yourself. Make the best choice today!

God, please help me use my freedom to make good choices.

47

God Knows Everything

Our Lord is great and very powerful.
There is no limit to what he knows.

PSALM 147:5 ICB

God knows everything. He knows how you feel, what your dreams are, and everything about the world around you. If you ever have a question, ask God. Trust that the Holy Spirit will guide and teach you.

God, I am so glad you know everything and that you can teach me.

48

God Treasures You

The LORD your God has set you apart for himself. He has chosen you to be his special treasure.

DEUTERONOMY 7:6 NIRV

God treasures you above all the riches in the world. He loves you more than you can even understand. He knows everything about you and wants to spend time with you.

God, thank you that I am a treasure to you! That makes me feel so special.

God is on
your side.

49

God Shares with You

God did not spare his own Son. He gave him up for us all. Then won't he also freely give us everything else?

ROMAN 8:32 NIRV

Have you ever fought with someone over something you both wanted? God isn't like that. He shares everything—even his Son, Jesus. Look at the world he made to share with you and think about how you can share with others.

Thank you for showing me how to share, God.

50

God Delights in You

The LORD takes delight in those
who have respect for him.
They put their hope in his faithful love.

PSALM 147:11 NIRV

Everyone has done things that are good and things that are not so good. God is so delighted when you choose the right things. You fill him with joy when you trust in him.

God, help me to choose the right things. I want to bring you joy.

51

God Helps You Understand

Only the Lord gives wisdom.
Knowledge and understanding
come from him.

PROVERBS 2:6 ICB

God is always wise. He knows what you need and understands how you feel. You can ask him for help with anything. If there is something you are confused about, he can help you understand it.

God, thank you for helping me to understand.

52

God Is Dependable

Depend on the Lord.
Trust him, and he will take care of you.

PSALM 37:5 ICB

Trusting can be scary. It isn't always easy to trust. God is dependable. That means he is faithful to do everything he says he will do. You can trust him to take care of you.

I am so glad I can count on you, God.

God knows how
you feel.

55

God Blesses You When You Don't Quit

People who don't give up are blessed. You have heard that Job was patient. And you have seen what the Lord finally did for him.

JAMES 5:11 NIRV

Don't quit when things are hard. A man in the Bible named Job went through many difficult things. But he did not give up on God. Try to keep doing your best. God sees your hard work, and he will bless you for it.

God, please help me not to quit.

56

God Gives You Hope

May the God who gives hope
fill you with great joy.

ROMANS 15:13 NIRV

God will give you hope and joy when you put your trust in him. When he fills you with hope and joy, you can share it with other people.

God, thank you for giving me hope and joy. Help me to share it with others.

God sees you.

57

God Likes Being With You

"Let the little children come to me. Don't stop them, because the kingdom of heaven belongs to people who are like these children."

MATTHEW 19:14 ICB

Do you know God likes being with you? You can talk to him, make jokes with him, tell him stories, and share your dreams with him. You can also invite him to be with you when you are playing. He wants to be with you all the time!

Thank you, God, for being with me!

58

God Is Compassionate

The LORD is tender and kind. He is gracious. He is slow to get angry. He is full of love.

PSALM 103:8 NIRV

God cares about you. He understands why you feel a certain way, and he knows about your problems. He has a lot of compassion for you and always wants to help you.

Thank you for being compassionate and understanding, God.

59

God Gives Joy

You will fill me with joy
when I am with you.
You will make me happy forever
at your right hand.

PSALM 16:11 NIRV

God gives you a kind of joy that you can't get anywhere else or from anyone else. If you trust in God, he will bring you a life full of happiness and love.

Thank you, God, for filling me with joy and making me happy.

60

God Accepts You

"The Father gives me the people who are mine. Every one of them will come to me, and I will always accept them."

John 6:37 ICB

God will always accept you when you come to him. His arms are open, and he wants you to stay with him. He will never tell you to go away or leave him alone.

Thank you for wanting to be with me, God!

God's love
never ends.

61

God Knows When You Are Hurting

He doesn't forget the cries of those who are hurting.

PSALM 9:12 NIRV

Your parents probably hear you crying when you get hurt. God does too. He cares about you. If no one else notices your sadness, God does. He will always be with you.

Thank you, God, for caring about me when I am hurt.

62

God Helps You to Be Good

God is working in you to help you want to do what pleases him. Then he gives you the power to do it.

PHILIPPIANS 2:13 ICB

God doesn't expect you to be perfect. He knows you need help making good choices, and he is so proud of you when you do. He is ready to help when you need it.

God, I want to do what pleases you. Help me.

63

God Makes Things Go Well

"I'm giving you his rules and commands today. Obey them. Then things will go well with you and your children after you."

DEUTERONOMY 4:40 NIRV

God promises that if you obey him, then he will make things go well for you. Things won't always be easy, but God will work it all out for you in the end if you obey him.

God, thank you for making things go well for me.

64

God Supports You

"I will make you strong and will help you. I will support you with my right hand that saves you."

ISAIAH 41:10 ICB

Sometimes you might want a friend to play with or someone who just sits and listens to you. God is your very best support. He is always close and waiting to spend time with you. Ask him to help you today.

God, I am so grateful that you support me and make me strong.

God won't give up on you.

65

God Keeps His Promises

The LORD will keep all his promises.
He is faithful in everything he does.

PSALM 145:13 NIRV

God promises to love you, keep you safe, comfort you, bring you joy, and so much more. The best part is that you can trust him. He will keep his promises. Trust him and know that he will be faithful because he is a promise-keeper!

Thank you for keeping all your promises, God!

66

God Will Make Everything Right

The LORD works everything out
to the proper end.
Even those who do wrong were
made for a day of trouble.

PROVERBS 16:4 ICB

If someone has done something wrong to you, and it still hasn't been made right, don't worry. God will make everything right in the end. Let go of the things you can't control, and trust God to fix it all.

Thank you, God, for making all things right.

67

God Saves You from Your Fears

I asked the Lord for help,
and he answered me.
He saved me from all that I feared.

Psalm 34:4 ICB

When you are full of fear, turn to God. He will comfort you and bring you peace. He will always be there for you. Remember that he is your refuge. He will keep you safe.

Thank you for saving me from my fears and protecting me, God!

68

God Works Everything for Good

We know that in everything God works for the good of those who love him. They are the people God called, because that was his plan.

Romans 8:28 ICB

God will take care of those who love him and give their lives to him. He has a plan for you. He will take care of you because he loves you and wants what is best for you. Trust him to work everything out for good.

God, I know you care about me. You will work everything out for good.

God gives you what you need.

69

God Will Fight Your Battles

"The LORD will fight for you. Just be still."

EXODUS 14:14 NIRV

God is your weapon. You will never lose a battle with him on your side. He is the strongest and most courageous warrior. Take your battles to God and ask him to fight for you. He will because he loves you.

Thank you for fighting my battles and winning them for me, God!

70

God Pays Attention to You

The LORD will watch over your life
no matter where you go,
both now and forever.

PSALM 121:8 NIRV

God is always paying attention. He watches over you. He knows how to take good care of you, and he always will. You don't need to try to get his attention; you already have it!

God, thank you for always paying attention to me.

71

God Is Faithful

Even if we are not faithful, he remains faithful. He must be true to himself.

2 TIMOTHY 2:13 NIRV

You can put your faith in God because he is faithful. That means he will never fail you. He will always do what he says he is going to do. He keeps all his promises.

Thank you, God, for being so faithful.

72

God Is Right

What the LORD says is right and true.
He is faithful in everything he does.

PSALM 33:4 NIRV

God knows everything. Everything he says is true. He will do what is right in your life, and he will help you make great choices if you trust in him.

God, you are right! I trust you.

God is real.

73

God Gives You a Purpose

"I have good plans for you. I don't plan to hurt you. I plan to give you hope and a good future."

JEREMIAH 29:11 ICB

God put you on this earth for a reason. He knows what is best for you, and he has a purpose for your life. Trust and know that what he has planned for you is good.

God, thank you for giving me a purpose.

74

God's Love Will Not Go Away

*"The mountains may disappear,
and the hills may come to an end.
But my love will never disappear."*

ISAIAH 54:10 ICB

God always loves you. There is never a day that he won't love you. He loves you during good times and bad. His love for you will never ever go away.

God, thank you for your love that never leaves!

75

God Will Take Care of Your Needs

"The thing you should want most is God's kingdom and doing what God wants. Then all these other things you need will be given to you."

MATTHEW 6:33 ICB

God has done so much for you. He has given you everything you need. When you live for him, you ask for the things that he wants for you. And then you can be sure he will give you those things!

God, thank you for taking care of everything I need.

76

God Is Forgiving

"When you stand praying, forgive anyone you have anything against. Then your Father in heaven will forgive your sins."

MARK 11:25 NIRV

God has forgiven you for everything you have done wrong. He asks you to forgive others in the same way. Think of a time when someone did something mean to you and ask God to help you forgive that person.

God, please help me to forgive others like you forgive me.

God made you special.

77

God Takes Away Your Sin

"I have swept away your sins like a big cloud. I have removed your sins like a cloud that disappears into the air."

ISAIAH 44:22 ICB

When you ask God to forgive you, he takes away all your sin. He makes all the bad things you've done disappear like a cloud in the sky. Thank him for sweeping your sin away with the clouds.

God, thank you for taking away my sin.

78

God Will Tell You Great Things

"Call out to me. I will answer you. I will tell you great things you do not know. And unless I do, you wouldn't be able to find out about them."

JEREMIAH 33:3 NIRV

God has so many great things to tell you! There is nothing he does not know. Ask him to tell you about the wonderful things he has created and done.

God, thank you for the great things you can tell me all about!

79

God Gives Generously

God can give you more blessings than you need. Then you will always have plenty of everything. You will have enough to give to every good work.

2 CORINTHIANS 9:8 ICB

God has blessed you more than you could ever know. He has given you new life through Jesus' work on the cross! The best way you can give back to God for all he has done is to give him your time and attention.

God, thank you for giving so generously!

80

God Rewards Respect

Respecting the Lord and not being proud will bring you wealth, honor and life.

PROVEBRS 22:4 ICB

When you choose to respect God and follow his ways, he rewards you with wealth, honor, and life. Sometimes it is hard to admit that you don't know everything. God doesn't expect you to! He just wants you to trust him and follow where he leads you.

God, help me to respect you with my choices.

81

God Is Powerful

Lord, you are great and powerful.
Glory, majesty and beauty belong to you.

1 Chronicles 29:11 NIRV

God is great and powerful. All the beautiful things on the earth belong to him because he made them all. Look outside at some of the things he has created and thank him for them.

God, you are great and powerful. Thank you for creating this world and everything in it.

82

God Gives Good Gifts

"Even though you are bad, you know how to give good gifts to your children. So surely your heavenly Father will give good things to those who ask him."

MATTHEW 7:11 ICB

God loves his children so much. He is good and he knows just what you need. God will bless you with many things because he cares for you. He listens to your prayers.

God, I am thankful that you know exactly what I need, and you bless me with so much.

God has a purpose for you.

83

God Watches Over Your Sleep

I can lie down and go to sleep.
And I will wake up again
because the Lord protects me.

Psalm 3:5 ICB

Do you sometimes feel afraid when you go to bed? A dark room can feel scary and lonely. You don't have to be afraid because God is watching over you always. He will help you sleep and he will stay with you when you wake up.

God, thank you for taking care of me even when I sleep.

84

God Is the King Forever

The Lord rules forever.
He sits on his throne to judge.

PSALM 9:7 ICB

God has been the King since before the beginning of time. He will always be the King. You can trust that he will rule his kingdom in the very best way. He is kind, fair, and just. Give honor to God the King today!

God, you are my King forever! Thank you for being a ruler who always does what is right.

85

God Holds You

*"Do not be afraid. I am with you.
I will hold you safe in my hands."*

ISAIAH 41:10 NIRV

God is with you. He holds you in his hands. He will keep you safe and bring you peace. You do not have to ever feel afraid or alone because he is always close.

Thank you for holding me in your hand, God.

86

God Is Holy

"You must be holy, because I am holy."

1 PETER 1:16 ICB

God is holy. This means he has never done anything wrong. He always makes the right choice. He is always good. He is always honest and fair. You can be holy because Jesus died on the cross to take away your sin. Ask God to help you be holy.

God, thank you for being holy. I honor you today.

87

God Is Gentle

*"Accept my work and learn from me.
I am gentle and humble in spirit."*

MATTHEW 11:29 ICB

God protects the hearts of those he loves. He is humble and gentle, and he knows how to speak to you in these ways. You can feel his peace just by talking to him. Do not be afraid. He is gentle and kind to his children.

Thank you for being gentle with me, God. I feel your peace when you speak to me.

88

God Sings Over You

"He will take great delight in you. In his love he will no longer punish you. Instead, he will sing for joy because of you."

ZEPHANIAH 3:17 NIRV

God loves spending time with you. He loves who you are. You are his joy and his delight. He sings because of you. The God of all creation finds joy in you! That is pretty special.

God, thank you for singing over me. I am glad I make you happy.

God rewards
hard work.

89

God Will Give You Good Advice

"I will guide you and teach you
the way you should go.
I will give you good advice
and watch over you with love."

PSALM 32:8 NIRV

If you don't know the best choice to make, you can always pray and ask God. He knows what is best and he will show you the right way to go. His advice is always good.

Thank you for always telling me what is right, God.

90

God Wants You to Ask

"Remain in me and follow my teachings. If you do this, then you can ask for anything you want, and it will be given to you."

JOHN 15:7 ICB

God is always listening to you. He wants to hear your questions. Even if you think your question is silly, do not be afraid to ask. God loves when you ask him questions.

God, thank you for listening to my questions!

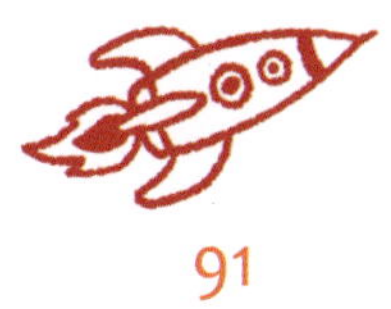

God Will Protect Your Spirit

The Lord is faithful. He will give you strength and protect you from the Evil One.

2 THESSALONIANS 3:3 ICB

God will keep your spirit safe. You do not have to be afraid. God is with you, and he will watch over you. He will guard you from the lies and plans of the devil. Your spirit is safe with God.

Thank you, God, for protecting my spirit.

92

God Wins

"In this world you will have trouble. But be encouraged! I have won the battle over the world."

JOHN 16:33 NIRV

God doesn't promise that living in this world will be easy. But you can have courage because he has already won the battle. There is nothing that is impossible with him. Stick with God, and you will always win!

God, thank you that you have already won the battle. I want to stay on your side.

93

God Loves Everyone

"God so loved the world that he gave his one and only Son. Anyone who believes in him will not die but will have eternal life."

JOHN 3:16 NIRV

God sent his Son, Jesus, to die for your sin because he loves you. He did this for every single person! He wants to spend eternity with all his children. Choose to follow him and love others well today.

God, please help me to love everyone like you do.

94

God Will Not Forget You

"Be strong and brave. Don't be afraid of them. Don't be frightened. The Lord your God will go with you. He will not leave you or forget you."

DEUTERONOMY 31:6 ICB

God will never forget you. He promises to protect you and stay with you. He said he will be with you at all times, so you can trust that he will.

God, thank you for never forgetting about me.

God is kind.

95

God Will Deliver You

"Call out to me when trouble comes.
I will save you. And you will honor me."

PSALM 50:15 NIRV

Call out to God and he will deliver you from your troubles. He will take care of you if you trust in him. God will be with you during hard times, and he will help you to get out of them. Thank him today for helping you.

God, thank you for delivering me from trouble and fear.

96

God Is Full of Peace

God's peace will keep your hearts and minds in Christ Jesus. The peace that God gives is so great that we cannot understand it.

PHILIPPIANS 4:7 ICB

God can give you peace because he is full of it! When you feel afraid or upset, God can bring you his peace. Just talking to him will help you feel better. If you are feeling upset right now, ask God to give you his peace.

I am so grateful for the peace you give me, God.

97

God Gives You Wisdom

If any of you needs wisdom, you should ask God for it. He will give it to you. God gives freely to everyone and doesn't find fault.

JAMES 1:5 NIRV

When you don't know what to do, ask God for help. He always knows what is best. Ask God for wisdom and he will give it to you.

Thank you, God, for giving me wisdom when I don't know what to do.

98

God Makes You Healthy

Don't depend on your own wisdom.
Respect the Lord and refuse to do wrong.
Then your body will be healthy.

PROVERBS 3:7-8 ICB

Try your best to do what's right and stop doing what is wrong. Show God that you respect him, and he will help keep your mind and body healthy.

God, help me to be healthy by making good choices.

99

God Has a Place for You

"There are many rooms in my Father's house. I would not tell you this if it were not true. I am going there to prepare a place for you."

JOHN 14:2 NIRV

After Jesus rose from the dead, he went back to heaven and prepared a place for you. There's a room ready for you in God's house. There is a special place for you! Isn't that exciting?

Jesus, thank you for preparing a room for me in God's house.

100

God Lights the Way

Your word is like a lamp
that shows me the way.
It is like a light that guides me.

PSALM 119:105 NIRV

The Bible is full of God's words that teach, warn, and guide you. It's like a book of instructions that lights up the path for the best way to live. He can help you follow his path.

God, thank you for lighting the way for me.